Mindful Thoughts

Medha Pahi

BookLeaf Publishing

India | USA | UK

Presentation by *BookLeaf Publishing*

Web: www.bookleafpub.com

E-mail: info@bookleafpub.com

ISBN: 9789360948535

First edition 2024

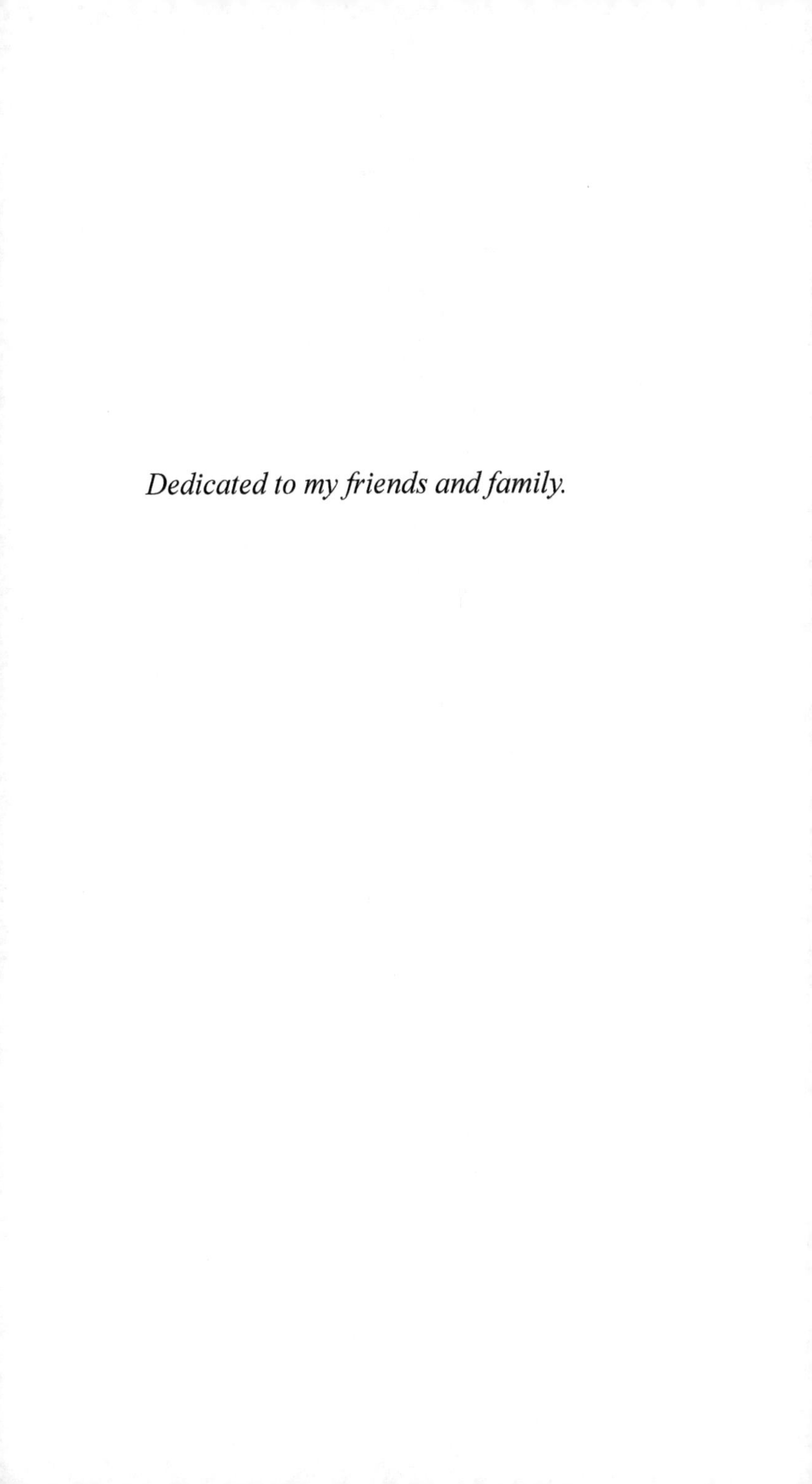

Dedicated to my friends and family.

A Streak of Hope

One blue spot
On a dark cloudy day
Sticking out and reminding us
There is hope
All bad times are temporary
Good times await to come
Everything will be alright
This is a sign from the universe
It's like a hand of reassurance
A streak of hope
Light after dark
Happiness after grief
Flowers after a storm
Sunrise after a dark night
Stay strong,

Shield

I wish I had shield to protect me
Words are the cruelest weapon
Cutting deeper than any wound
Hard to heal from
Unlike physical pain words tend to stay
A shield would've been great
Instead of feeling like a soldier with no weapon
Powerless
Easy target
Horrifically waiting to be aimed at
All hearts deserve a shield
We all are fighting our own battles
Even cruelty has its limits
But strength outweighs it,

Rage

Did I mean nothing to you?
Why did you walk away?
Did you never think of me?
I gave you so many chances
You were my best friend
I never did anything
It was all you
I don't regret meeting you
I just wonder
Would it have been better if stayed strangers
I should've listened to my friends
They were right
You meant so much to me
I would've never walked away
Perhaps in the future we can try again,

Final Goodbye

I decided to let your memory fade
No matter how hard I try
You won't come back
Your absence will always be an unhealed wound
No bandage can fix
I waited forever
For things to change
You were a great lesson
I don't regret meeting you
At one point only you bought a smile to my face
How can you move on so easily
I'm still picking up the pieces
I wish you were here still
I want to tell you so much
I will always cherish our time together
I hope all the best for you
If you have a change of heart
I'll be here
Just like always,

Grave

The day I found out you were gone
Is the day my body went numb
My heart shattered into pieces
Wishing I could say goodbye
Hear your voice again
Laugh with you again
I wish you told me about your struggles
Can't walk through the halls the same
I'll always see your face
I miss you
I hope heaven is happy
I didn't think it'd be over so soon
The memories hurt
The endless tears
Grief is horrible
I just want 5 more mins
I hate how permanent death is
A scar so deep
The pain so heavy
Till the day we meet again,

2:15 a.m

I woke up one night
Without a nightmare or anything
Just laying in the dark
Thinking about life
The moon shined so bright
The stars sparkled
The snow glowed
The peace was oddly comforting
The hours where nothing is expected of you
You can just lie there
In the quiet alone with your thoughts
No questions asked
The night is much more peaceful
All alone
Thinking as freely as you desire
Letting your imagination run wild
It's the best time to do a reflection on your day
Possibly find solutions to your problems
Feeling every emotion possible,

Painted Sky

As I sit on the cool sand
Watching the waves rise and fall
The sky appears to be a painting
Full of many colors
Bursting across
Pink mixing with orange, purple, yellow, red,and
an ombre mix
While the golden sun sinks to blend in with the
ocean
Creating an everlasting, breathtaking view
Hearing the birds chirp
Animals taking their shelters
Eventually the sky goes dark
And the stars shimmer
Marking the end of the day,

Blossoms

What truly marks the end of winter?
The sight of the first blooming flower
Here to stay until fall
The beautiful golden yellow one
Growing after the seasonal rain
Blossoming everywhere you go
Making a home for the bees
And the earthly scent
Children picking bouquets
And blowing dandelions
As the never ending rain
Brings more types of flowers
Creating a natural palette
Of long lasting beauty
Each season more gorgeous than the previous
As we await for many more,

Forever Flame

Hikes always lead to a destination
But some lead to unknown mysteries
Crossing an obstacle of fallen trees
Crawling and squeezing through some
Old dry leaves
Slippery and muddy paths
Some scraped knees
With rainy weather
Branches and rocks
Lots of walking and sometimes falling
Leading to a tree hollow
With a sparkling orange flame
 No origin of how it was lit
And nothing to blow it out
Completely unaffected by bad weather
Burning in the best condition
Truly a once in a life experience,

Strangers

When it was meant to be forever
Why didn't it last?
We were so close
Truly the best of friends
I still remember the day we met
How instantly we clicked
One conversation led to countless memories
But in a flash it was all gone
How?
We promised each other so much
But like fragile glass they all broke
On a random day
I sat in shock
Wondering the true reason why
Wishing I could ask you
I still think of us so often
Do you think of me?
What was and what could've been
Maybe one day we'll talk again
Really understand why
But until then
I hope you accomplish all the things you wanted
to
And are happy
I'll always be here waiting,
For one more day of us,

Time That Won't Come Back

Remember when we were in elementary school?
Just waiting to go to recess
Our happy squeals
Wild imaginations
So many friends
Fun slides
 Competitions on the swings
Four square
Hula hoops
Jump ropes
The dread of recess ending
Why does childhood only happen once?

Which One's the Brake and Speed?

It was finally the day I started to drive
My dad explained what each function was
How to work the shift
Adjust the mirrors
The right and left turn signals
Which one's the brake and speed
I started the car
And tried my hardest to put the car in drive
Such a simple thing felt so difficult
I had a huge fear of reaching the max speed
Even though I only pressed it a little
I remember slamming the brake
My hands and legs trembling
Thinking how am I ever going to learn
Eventually I did
It took a lot patience and effort
But now it is really simple
Yet now I realize the precious time spent with
my parents,

Last Leaf

The dry old wrinkly leaf
Hanging all alone
Waiting for the wind
To blow it off
Wishing it had one other leaf to talk to
So it wouldn't have to die all alone
Once a whole tree full of many green leaves
Watching each change color
Then eventually meeting its fate
Wishing that it could go too
Reminiscing the great times the seasons bought
Never to be experienced again
 Not knowing when and if they'd meet again
Wishing for 5 more minutes
To say departing words
And to be together one last time,

Stuffed Animals

You ask your parents for a new stuffed animal
you liked
They say yes
You're overjoyed
Deciding its name
Your adventures
Making your stuffy a small plate of your meal
Watch cartoons together
Play board games
Read your fav book
Go on trips
Make clothes,
Even want to go to school with it
After sometime
You move on to a different animal
Deep down you remember all those memories
and care
 Now you're no longer carefree
Always dreaming about how amazing those
times were
And how you took it for granted
A tear rolls down your cheek,

A New City

It's time to sell the house you grew up in
The first one where you came as a newborn
Took your first steps
Said your first words
Went to pre-school in
Drew on the walls
Graduated high school
Came for each holiday
Spent countless hours playing outside
Made all of your friends
Experienced the good and bad
Memorized each corner
Standing in your childhood bedroom
Seeing how far you've come
And realize that you won't sleep in it again
Take a final drive around your hometown
Not knowing when you'll come back
In the morning the movers will come and take
everything
So you'll have to go too
To a new city with no one you know
Starting over
Hoping it's all going to be worth it,

Better Off

Maybe I'm better off without you in my life
I truly deserved more
Than a cruel goodbye
I spent so long asking myself why
I even took the blame
When it wasn't my fault
I wish I didn't waste my life
My energy
On someone who couldn't care less
I was just a person to you
But to me you meant so much
Life is honestly so peaceful
Without your spears
I'm glad our chapter closed
Sometimes think it should've ended sooner
I've found peace
And better friends
Some people are truly a lesson
A hurtful one
But so necessary
Glad I got to see your true colors,

New Kid

I left my home country behind
To start a new life
And to have better opportunities
I went to a very different school
Not one thing was similar
The clothes, food, priorities
The hardest one was the language barrier
Not understanding what was being said
Without a translator
People laughed at me
Mocked and snickered
Still I was a lot better than them in classes
No one last minute studies
Like I do
I went home to a rich culture and traditions
I was really ambitious
And kept my head up
I miss my home and family often
But am grateful for the new opportunities I will
have,

A Blank Book

We all start off with an unwritten book
Our life experiences are what is scribbled all
over it
Some brighten the pages
While others crumple it
Everything we do is written
Regardless of being small
Most of the time we decide what is put on them
Sometimes we don't get a choice
There is a path for everyone in life
A new page for each opportunity
It might not seem like it's our favor
Eventually all things work out
As we grow older
One by one each chapter of life closes
We long to go back to a chapter
We're all authors
Even though we haven't written books
The story of my life
Exists within us all,

Our Strengths

Setbacks are bound to happen in life
Having the courage to keep going
Is what truly makes us strong
Everyday we face some sort of fear
Our bravery pushes us through it
We fight our inner demons
Not letting bad thoughts possess us
Enduring pain is a like a spear
Our heart feels it and tries to remove the wound
Some spears cut deeper than others
 Yet we eventually move on
Time is something we always want more of
But try to make the best of what was given
Our morals and ethics are going to be questioned
How we hold to them is what outcome we will
face
The strength to always run to the finish line
Is the greatest gift we can give ourselves,

Greater Decisions

I often think of the day
A better choice could've been made
The outcome more sufficient
And what I hoped for
Yet the fault at the time
Filled me with deep guilt
The desire to go back
And change the occurrence
Clawed at me daily
Time passed
It stung less
But remained a late night thought
I know I tried my best
Or so I thought
The event became a lesson
To reflect upon as I aged,

Stadium

Thousands upon thousands of people
Cheering for one thing
All of their happiness poured into their team's
performance
 Yet it is probably the only thing each person has
in common
We're all so different
But sometimes we all stand together
Just like a community
All of us are humans
Everyone has solitary thoughts and experiences
We all hold our own values
No two people are the same
Uniqueness is what truly makes the world better
All similarities would be repetitive and dull
Good differences make life livable
We see and hear so many perspectives
But our mind forms our own
Making us who we are meant to be,